K now Your Cats

Jack
Byard

Old Pond Publishing

GW00648233

First published 2013

ISBN 978-1-908397-60-7

A catalogue record for this book is available from the British Library

Published by
Old Pond Publishing Ltd
Dencora Business Centre
36 White House Road
Ipswich IP1 5LT
United Kingdom

www.oldpond.com

Book design by Liz Whatling
Printed and bound in China

Contents

Acknowledgements

Many thanks to all the cat lovers and breeders for all their help and of course the beautiful photographs they have allowed me to use. The stories and conversations about their much-loved cat families have been an inspiration. I grudgingly accept that any mistakes are mine and that my grand-daughter Rebecca and my young friends Sophie and Lauren are blameless, at least as far as the cats are concerned. And last but not least thanks to all the staff of Old Pond Publishing who keep me in gainful and honest employment.

Picture Credits

(1) Matt Hoskins, *(2)* Leon Mitchell, *(3)* Gregory Moulard Muscapix, *(4)* ©Olivier Delaere, *(5)* David Belleville, *(6)* Richard Walker, *(7)* June Payne, *(8)* Marlies Koorenneef, Nimble Nymph Cattery, *(9)* H. Cuervo, *(10)* Carsten Reisinger, *(11)* Ingela Ring, *(12)* Bion Kirk, Junglemtnexotics.com, *(13)* Shoenweg Camila Blanchfleur, Ermine Trace Cattery, Russia, *(14)* Michelle Penney, *(15)* Daniel Pierce and Kuo Chen Huang, Maunarch Egyptian Maus, *(16)* Chiara Bagnoli, *(17)* Susan Booth susanbooth2@aol.com, *(18)* Ayshazen Burmese & Khao Manee Cats, *(19)* Nick Kenrick, *(20)* Krister Parmstrand, *(21)* Natalia Solopova, *(22)* Iain Burke, *(23)* Loes van der Zande, *(24)* Karen Edland, *(25)* Markus Wagner, *(26)* Brad Francis Photography, *(27)* Alsoomse Pixie Bobs, *(28)* Tara Rerrie, *(29)* L. Spruit, twinkledolls, Netherlands, *(30)* Brooke Wilton, *(31)* Ineta McParland, *(32)* Damian Weed, Just Cats Veterinary Hospital, *(33)* Owner Trinette Marriott, breeder Sue Bell, photo Louis Paul Photography, *(34)* Kreative Capture, tesoro@prodigy.com, *(35)* Clare Ferris-Druzhina Siberians, *(36)* Lil Shepherd, *(37)* Wally Hooker, *(38)* Robin Hao Gonzalez Photography, *(39)* 'Caviar' owned by Anna Leskowsky, *(40)* 'Luna' by Laura Ringsell, *(41)* Xavier Billard.

Foreword

Our ever-loving feline friends or, dare I say it, moggies, have the undeserved reputation of being aloof. Far from it – they are loving companions, intelligent and always playful, and prepared to sit on your lap and listen to your troubles and triumphs, only talking when necessary. A perfect companion. My own domestic was small and all-black. But when a Border collie puppy arrived, Dinkie let it be known that she was the boss with a smart smack on young Jock's nose with a small black paw. And so it was for over thirteen years' companionship to me and with each other.

Cats have travelled a long and sometimes difficult road from the early days of history, but they also reached great heights, often being revered as higher beings. The working cat, brought to this country by the Romans, undertook the necessary task of keeping vermin at bay. The domestic cat of today is companion, vermin exterminator and patient listener all in one.

To me it is sad that many of the cats mentioned in this book are 'house cats' and never have the freedom of an un-fenced garden or to see the blue skies. They have a total lack of road sense, seeing no danger in speeding traffic. Their trusting nature makes them easy prey for thieves, to be sold on as an elegant pet or to an unscrupulous breeder. Do the thieves ever stop to think of the distress they cause? Of course not – that would be foolish!

Jack Byard 2013

1.

Abyssinian

Weight:
4 to 7.5 kg (9–16.5 lb)

Lifespan:
14 to 17 years

The coat is soft and silky. The colour most often seen, and called 'Usual', is a warm reddish-brown, with black tips to each hair known as 'ticking'. The ears are large and the nose is tile-red. The almond-shaped eyes can be gold, green, hazel and copper, depending on coat colours which include sorrel, blue and lilac.

The breed is believed to have come from Abyssinia, now Ethiopia, brought in 1868 to the UK by Captain Barrett Lennard's wife who sailed with her husband. The cat named Zula was the first Aby in the British Isles. Although it was believed at one time they were descendants of the ancient cats of Egypt they are more likely to have come from the east coast of Ethiopia, before it became landlocked. In the early 20th century, before vaccinations, the breed was decimated by leukaemia.

The Aby makes a highly intelligent and loving companion.

Balinese

Weight:
2.5 to 5 kg (5.5–11 lb)

Lifespan:
9 to 15 years

Description

Similar in appearance to a Siamese, the Balinese is slim, lithe and graceful with vivid blue eyes. Its colours – blue, lilac, seal and chocolate with the addition of red, cream and tabby – are also similar to the Siamese, but its soft ermine-like coat is much longer.

There are numerous theories as to the origins of the Balinese, with many twists and turns to its history. Many believe the Balinese is a long-haired mutation of the Siamese or possibly a domestic variation of the Pallas or Manul cat from western China. Yet another possibility is the result of the crossing of the Siamese with the Turkish Angora that arrived in the western world of the 14th century, courtesy of the Crusaders. The truth is most likely a combination of all these. The breeding and showing of the Balinese was started in earnest in 1955 by Marion Dorsey of California.

This playful, intelligent cat will actively seek out human companionship.

Bengal

Weight:
5.5 to 9 kg (12– 20 lb)

Lifespan:
12 to 16 years

Description

The Bengal has a thick coat with a glitter-like sheen. Its colours are brown, seal lynx point, mink, sepia or silver with spotted and marbled patterns. The spots can be solid, arrow-shaped or as rosettes. The eyes are blue, gold, copper, green, bronze, brown and hazel, depending on the coat colour.

The Bengal life began in Yuma, Arizona in 1963. Dr Willard Centerwall of the University of California had been carrying out unsuccessful research into transferring to the domestic cat the Asian Leopard cat's apparent immunity to feline leukaemia. Jean Mill-Sugden, herself a geneticist, obtained eight of these cats from Dr Willard as the basis for breeding the Bengal. One of Jean's aims was to offer an alternative to keeping illegal and increasingly at-risk wild cats. With the help of Dr Greg Kent, careful crossing and breeding, success was finally achieved.

In 1984 these beautiful, playful, loving animals were accepted as domestic cats.

4.

Birman

Weight:
4.5 to 8 kg (10–17.6 lb)

Lifespan:
11 to 15 years

The background body colors are eggshell or golden and the two main point colours, the originals out of twenty, are seal point and blue point. The silky hair is semi-long. The Birman comes with a bushy tail, four white gloves and round, deep blue eyes.

The Birman legend begins before the birth of Buddha. The devout Kymer people of Burma built magnificent temples and a gold statue to honour the goddess Tsun-Kyan-Kse. The temple was attacked by robbers and when the priest Mun-Ha was killed, his cat leapt to his defence and absorbed the soul of the priest. The cat transformed into a Birman Seal Point, seen as a sign from the goddess, whereupon the remaining priests drove the thieves from the temple. For the next seven days the cat did not eat or drink, and died taking both their souls to paradise. Overnight all the temple cats were transformed into beautiful Birmans. A wonderful legend!

Bombay

Weight:
2.7 to 5.6 kg (6–11 lb)

Lifespan:
13 to 15 years

Description

The all-black velvet coat is tight and close-lying. The Bombay has black or brown paw pads and large copper-coloured eyes.

The Bombay is a designer cat produced in the mid 1950s, a cross of the Burmese with either a Black British or American Shorthair. The sole intention of the American breeder, Nikki Horner of Louisville, Kentucky, was to create a domestic cat that looked like a miniature panther and so it is nicknamed the 'parlour panther'. As kittens they have a tendency to be timid but as they mature their personality bursts through. This is not your typical nose-in-the-air independent – they are not known as the 'Velcro cat' for nothing, staying close to one member of the family throughout the day.

They are full of energy and love to play games. They crave attention, love to snuggle up and are good with children. Do not feed snacks, however persuasive they are. Diabetes through over-eating can be a problem.

British Longhair

Weight:
3.6 to 8 kg (8–18 lb)

Lifespan:
14 to 20 years

Description

The British Longhair has a dense coat that stands out from the body, in most colours with blue being the most popular. Its head is round with chubby cheeks and a short nose. Eyes are blue or green depending on coat colour

The British Longhair is a possibly a development of the British Shorthair brought to Britain by the Romans in the 2nd century AD. Before that they were favourites of the Egyptian emperors. In both cases their main purpose in life was to keep the grain stores free of vermin. Another school of thought suggests instead that its development began in England at the latter end of the 19th century. Is this a man-made breed or an old, yet long-ignored breed? The debate will no doubt continue for another thousand years. Strangely, the BLH is not recognised as a separate breed in this country.

In the United States it is known as the Lowlander and in Europe the Britannica.

British Shorthair

Weight:
3.4 to 7.7 kg (7.5–17 lb)

Lifespan:
10 to 20 years

Description

This medium-sized cat comes in over 30 colours, the blue being the most popular. The large round eyes are green, hazel or gold depending on body colour.

The British Shorthair was officially acknowledged in 1889, but the shorthair cat is believed to have arrived in the British Isles hundreds of years before with the Roman invaders. These were working cats earning their living keeping in check the rodent population. Once happy to roam dark alleys taking care of business and sleeping in odd corners, they now prefer the home comforts of a settee and a warm fire. The credit for the breed's development in the 19th century is given to Harrison Weir who searched for the best of these working cats and created a pedigree breed. They made their public debut in 1871 at the first-ever cat show, organised by Harrison Weir and held in the Crystal Palace, London.

A calm, gentle yet independent companion.

Burmese

Weight:
3.5 to 6.5 kg (8–14.3 lb)

Lifespan:
10 to 16 years

Description

The main colours of the slim, elegant, compact and well-muscled Burmese are brown, blue, lilac, chocolate, cream and red plus all the above with added cream called 'torti'. The eyes are varying shades of yellow or gold.

The majority of Burmese cats are descended from Wong Mau who, in 1930, was brought to America from Burma by Dr Joseph Cheesman Thompson. It was originally believed that the Burmese was little more than another variation of the Siamese, a theory that was hotly disputed by Dr Thompson. Research carried out by two biologists, Billie Gerst and Virginia Cobb, and geneticist Dr Clyde Keeler proved that the Burmese was an independent breed. The kittens develop their final colour as they mature and originally all Burmese cats were dark brown.

They are social, intelligent, curious, playful and very naughty, well into old age. They are ideal for crowded households and a good friend for children.

Burmilla

Weight:
4 to 7 kg (9–15.4 lb)

Lifespan:
13 to 17 years

Description

The elegant-looking Burmilla has a rounded head and a short, dense silky coat. The coat can be shaded or tipped; the colours are black, blue, chocolate-brown and lilac. The lips and nose have pencilled outline, as do the green eyes.

The Burmilla is the result of a chance meeting, in England in 1980, between a male silver Chinchilla and a female lilac Burmese. The four resultant female kittens were, according to all accounts, gorgeous. The owner called a friend, Baroness Miranda von Kirchberg who, instead of turning her back on nature's mistake, decided to breed from them and create a breed that had the beautiful colouring of the Chinchilla and the shape, coat and the superb temperament of the Burmese – the best of both worlds. Within four years the breed standard was agreed and the breed was officially recognised.

The owners tell me they are good-tempered, playful, affectionate and enjoy human company.

Calico

Weight:
3.2 to 4.1 kg (7–9 lb)

Lifespan:
12 to 18 years

Description

The Calico is usually white, brown, black and orange. The eyes can be any colour.

This is not, despite popular belief, a breed. Calico refers to a coloured pattern on the fur that is mainly found in the Manx, British, American and Exotic Shorthairs, Persian, Turkish Van and Japanese Bobtail breeds. It is known as Tortoiseshell and White in the British Isles and Europe while paler varieties go by the name of Clouded Tigers. The Calico effect is linked to the X chromosome and the majority of Calico cats are female. Only one in three thousand is male and they are usually sterile. While studying the migration patterns of domestic cats, Neil Todd discovered that the Calico originated in Egypt from where it migrated to the Mediterranean ports of Italy, Spain and France.

Many cultures in history have believed that Calico cats have magical powers and Japanese sailors adopted them to bring good luck. In America it is known as the 'money' cat.

Chartreux

Weight:
2.7 to 6.8 kg (6–15 lb)

Lifespan:
13 to 16 years

Description

The thick woolly coat can be any shade of blue-grey. The head is round with full cheeks; the large round eyes are copper to gold, brilliant orange being preferred. The overall look is described as a 'potato on toothpicks'.

This rare breed from France is also known as the smiling cat from France because the rounded shape of the head and the soft expressive eyes give the impression of a Mona Lisa smile. The first documented mention of the breed was made in the 18th century by the biologist Comte de Buffon. Although the Chartreux looks at first sight to be similar to the blue British Shorthair, modern research suggests that it began its life in Persia, modern Iran. In the 13th century the ancestors of the Chartreux arrived in France with returning Crusaders who took them to the Grande Chartreux Monastery outside Paris.

The national cat of France, this breed was a favourite of French President Charles de Gaulle.

Chausie

Weight:
6 to 11.5 kg (13.2–25.4 lb)

Lifespan:
13 to 18 years

Description

The Chausie is long, tall and lean, just like me. The coat is short, black, black-grizzled, tabby and a black, brown, ticked tabby. The eyes, oval at the bottom and flat at the top, are gold or yellow.

It is thought that hybrids between the wild jungle cat *(Felis chaus)* and the domestic cat *(Felis catus)* may have appeared in Egypt several thousand years ago. The Chausie is a modern exotic hybrid along the same lines. It was created in the 1960s – the cross of a jungle cat and the Abyssinian – designed to fill the desire to own a wild cat but with the domestic cat's behavioral traits, in other words its safety. I understand that the latest generation of this controlled breeding programme are 'fully domestic compliant'. I don't think the EU is involved, yet.

Intelligent and active, the Chausie cannot wait for playtime. If you enjoy the wild look this is the cat for you – and it is hamster friendly.

Chinchilla

Weight:
3.5 to 5.4 kg (7.7–12 lb)

Lifespan:
12 to 15 years

The long, dense, silky white coat of the Chinchilla is tipped black, silver or gold giving a sparkly appearance. Their faces are round; the eyes are large and green or blue-green with brown rims like eyeliner. The round-tipped ears are tufted inside and the paws are large, round and tufted.

The first female Chinchilla, named Chinnie, was born in Wakefield, Yorkshire in 1882. Chinnie's mate was believed to be a tabby that was just passing through. Chinnie's offspring were to become prize- and medal-winners including 'Best in Show' at the Crystal Palace in 1886. Is the Chinchilla a new breed or just another variation of the 60-plus variations and colours of the Persian? The argument has raged for over a hundred years and shows no sign of abating. What is agreed is that the Chinnie is possibly the most beautiful longhair cat in existence.

The Chinnie is gentle and easy-going, preferring the comfort of an indoor life.

Cornish Rex

Weight:
2.5 to 4.4 kg (5.5–9.9 lb)

Lifespan:
11 to 15 years

Description

The Cornish Rex has sleek greyhound looks with a very fine down coat which can be lightly waved or rexing (curly), including eyebrows and whiskers. The range of coat and eye colours covers most known cat colours. The ears are large and tall, the eyes large and oval.

On 21 July 1950 on Bodmin Moor, Cornwall, Serena, a tortoiseshell cat, gave birth to a litter of five, one of which had a curly coat, a characteristic known in the cat world as 'rexing'. This kitten, Kallibunker, was the first Cornish Rex. The breeder, Mrs Nina Ennismore, contacted her veterinarian and geneticist A.C. Jude and a breeding programme was started. Further kittens were born but the gene pool was so small that before the breed was ten years old it was classed as endangered.

This is not an outdoor type, preferring to snuggle up somewhere warm on a lap or a blanket. The cats are full of fun and love company.

Egyptian Mau

Weight:
3.2 to 6.4 kg (7–14 lb)

Lifespan:
12 to 15 years

Description

The colours of the Egyptian Mau are silver, bronze and smoke with irregular spots and bands. The distinctive mascara lines on the face contribute to a worried expression. The nose of the silver and bronze is brick-red; the smoke has a black nose, and all have gooseberry-green eyes.

The Mau, possibly the oldest breed of cat, was domesticated between 3,000 and 2,000 BC, when harming a cat in Egypt was punishable by death.

In the 1930s an exiled Russian princess, Nathalie Troubetzkoy who had lived in England for 20 years, moved to Rome. There a young boy gave her a silver-spotted kitten that a diplomat had brought to the city from the Middle East. Intrigued by this elegant feline, Nathalie researched its ancestors and helped save its breed from extinction.

From earning its keep chasing mice and hunting birds, this fascinating and intelligent breed had developed to a prominent role in mythology and religion.

Exotic Shorthair

Weight:
3 to 6.5 kg (6.6–14.3 lb)

Lifespan:
12 to 15 years

Description

The Exotic Shorthair has a thick, plush coat. The head is broad and round with a short snub nose, and the ears are small with round tips. The eyes are large and round and can be blue, copper or green.

We owe the delights of the Exotic Shorthair to Carolyn Bussey an American cat breeder who, fifty years ago, crossed a Persian with a brown Burmese with the intention of creating a brown Persian. The result was a litter of black and extremely beautiful short-haired versions of a Persian. The inclusion of the American Shorthair created the gentle breed we know today, with over thirty patterns and colours including silver, lilac, chocolate and blue. To put it in a nutshell, it is a short-haired Persian requiring less grooming and shedding very little hair.

This gentle, lively, intelligent animal is a joy to be around, ideal for the young and not so young.

Havana

Weight:
3.2 to 4.5 kg (6–10 lb)

Lifespan:
10 to 15 years

Description

The Havana comes with a short smooth glossy coat in two colours: rich red-brown mahogany, and a pinkish-grey lilac, with matching whiskers. The round tips of the large ears tilt forward above brilliant green eyes.

In the 1950s Baroness Miranda Von Ullman and other breeders created the beautiful, intelligent and playful Havana. This was a new breed by design, a crossing of the chocolate and seal point Siamese with your basic short-haired domestic black cat. In 1958, after eight years of development, it was accepted by the Governing Council of the Cat Fancy as a new breed with the name 'Chestnut Foreign Shorthair'. Who thinks of these names? In 1970 the name was replaced by Havana because in colour, the brown resembled the Havana rabbit and the finest of Havana cigars.

Havanas have two favourite pastimes – playing and sleeping. Inquisitive to within an inch of their lives, at the slightest noise they will streak through the house to investigate.

Khao Manee

Weight:
3.6 to 4.5 kg (8–10 lb)

Lifespan:
10 to 12 years

Description

The pure white coat of the Khao Manee is short and smooth and the tail is long. The head is heart-shaped with high cheek bones, large upright ears, and eyes that are coloured from blue to yellow to green with a preference for odd-eye – one blue, one yellow.

The Khao Manee (meaning white gem), is not a hybrid or a man-made breed but a truly historic breed mentioned in the Thai *Cat-Book Poems* that date back to the 14th century. For many hundreds of years these could only be bred by members of the Thai Royal family. The Khao Manee is reputed to bestow good luck and longevity on the house where they live. This ancient breed is a newcomer to the western world, having arrived in 1999.

These muscular, athletic, intelligent cats have a great sense of fun and love to dash around playing fetch. They will then curl up on your lap.

Korat

Weight:
3.6 to 4.5 kg (8–10 lb)

Lifespan:
10 to 15 years

Description

The Korat has a fine silver-blue coat, each hair tipped with silver. Their nose and lips are dark blue or lavender, their ears are large with rounded tips. Their appearance can cast a spell – large eyes, luminous green with an amber cast, peering out from a blue heart-shaped face.

The Korat, named after a province in north-east Thailand, is an ancient breed dating back to at least the 13th century which has so far resisted the efforts of breeders to be 'improved'. Known colloquially as the 'good luck cat', it is traditionally given as a wedding gift to bestow good fortune and longevity. Their coats are said to 'resemble full rain clouds and their eyes shine like dew drops on a lotus leaf'. The kittens are born with blue eyes which over a period of 3–4 years turn luminous green. The popularity of the Korat began in the western world in the mid 20th century but it took many years before the breed was accepted by the breed organisations.

This is a great companion, loving and intelligent.

LaPerm

Weight:
3.5 to 5.4 kg (7.7–12 lb)

Lifespan:
10 to 15 years

The coat of the LaPerm is medium-long, curly-wavy and soft to the touch. Any colour is acceptable. The eye colours range from gold to aquamarine, including odd-eyed.

The beautiful Columbia River gorge, once home for many Native American tribes, is the birthplace of LaPerm. In 1982 on a cherry farm owned by Linda and Richard Koehl, a kitten was born with very little hair and when the hair grew it became curly, like a perm. 'Curly' was a Rex cat. Curly 'intermingled' with other farm cats; all the male kittens fathered other litters, and all had curly coats. A colony of curly haired cats was created. In naming the breed, Linda followed the native Chinookan tradition of mixing French with English where a pipe is 'lapeep'. So Curly's creation became LaPerm. When Linda took the cats to a show to ask advice, she was given tremendous support and the colony was used as the foundation for a new breed.

This is a loving, intelligent and playful lap cat.

Maine Coon

Weight:
4 to 10 kg (9–22 lb)

Lifespan:
13 to 16 years

Description

The long, shaggy coat of any colour is uneven with a soft downy undercoat and a glossy topcoat. The ears are large with tufted tips. The eyes can be shades of gold, copper or green

The history of the Maine Coon and its association with the American state of Maine goes back over 250 years with many myths and theories. The early owners are said to range from Marie Antoinette to Captain Charles Coon, an English seafarer. In truth it is most likely a mixture of breeds brought to America by the early settlers. It has possibly survived because it has not been 'improved' and has remained virtually as nature intended. Originally they worked on farms catching vermin. The thick shaggy coat acts as insulation in the harsh weather and if the cat becomes too cold it wraps its tail around like a blanket. It can take up to four years to mature.

An intelligent and affectionate companion.

Manx

Weight:
3.6 to 5.5 kg (8–12 lb)

Lifespan:
8 to 14 years

Description

The double coat of the Manx is soft and plush, the under coat is short and thick with a longer outer coat and it comes in a wide range of colours. The eyes are large and round, coloured gold to copper, blue, green, hazel and odd-eyed.

There are as many theories as to how the Manx arrived on the Isle of Man as there are stories as to why it has no tail. It could have been a survivor of the Spanish Armada shipwreck in 1588 or left behind by the Vikings. Or maybe Noah trapped the cat's tail when closing the door of the Ark! This is a genetic mutation created in part by the small gene pool because the breed was confined on a small island with inevitable in-breeding. Although a lack of tail became the norm, not all Manx cats are entirely tail-less. While the 'rumpy' has no tail at all, the 'stumpy' has a tail that is just visible and the 'longy' has a tail of over 5 cm (2 inches).

Forget the length of tail, they make wonderful pets.

Norwegian Forest

Weight:
3 to 9 kg (6.6–19.8 lb)

Lifespan:
15 to 18 years

Description

The Norwegian Forest comes in all known cat colours and patterns. It is a large cat with a dense double coat, a coarse outer coat with a woolly under coat making it virtually waterproof. It has tufted lynx-type ears, a ruff-like mane and a long bushy tail. The almond-shaped eyes are large and green-gold.

Here is another old, if not ancient, breed which some believe is descended from the Turkish Angora cats that traders brought to Norway and Europe and which bred with the local moggies. My belief is that they date back to the Vikings; in Viking myths and legends they were described as 'fairy cats'. Adapted to survive the harsh Norwegian climate, their impressive size made them superb vermin exterminators protecting grain stores on land and on Viking ships. They were regularly seen in European shows in the 1930s but it was several decades before they obtained full recognition.

Their gentle nature makes them ideal pets.

24

Ocicat

Weight:
2.5 to 6.5 kg (5.5–14.3 lb)

Lifespan:
10 to 15 years

Description

The smooth, short and lustrous coat comes in twelve colours with dark contrasting spots. All the hairs are ticked with the exception of the tail. The almond-shaped eyes are surrounded by dark fur and can be any colour except blue.

In 1964 American breeder Virginia Daly was attempting to create an Abyssinian Point Siamese. One of the litters contained a gorgeous golden-spotted kitten; Amanda's daughter said it looked like an Ocelot. This first Ocicat, Tonga, was neutered so was not truly the father of the breed but he was the spur needed to develop and create it. Other breeders joined the breeding programme, crossing the breeds used to produce Tonga in an attempt to re-create nature's blip. It took over 40 years for the Ocicat to reach championship status.

The Ocicat has looks of a wild cat but has the gentility of a domestic breed. They are an intelligent and friendly breed with a love of toys.

25

Oriental Longhair

Weight:
4 to 6.5 kg (9–14.3 lb)

Lifespan:
12 to 15 years

Description

This fine-boned breed has a sleek, silky draping coat, in approximately 300 colours. Its long, bushy tail is plume-like and its ears are large and wide. The almond-shaped eyes can be blue, green or one of each.

The Oriental Longhair is still reasonably rare. The original creation and development took place in England during the late 1950s by crossing the Balinese with an Oriental Shorthair. It was originally called the British Angora but was renamed in 2002 to avoid confusion with the Turkish Angora. It is said that when you stroke the Longhair it feels like stroking silk. It was imported into the USA in the 1970s where it has become one of the most popular breeds.

The breed has a winning personality – inquisitive and full of fun, they like to be involved in all that's going on. This is a companion for all the family: lively, talkative and intelligent, just like me.

26

Persian

Weight:
3.2 to 4.5 kg (7–10 lb)

Lifespan:
10 to 15 years

Description

The Persian's beautiful, long flowing coat, the longest of any breed, comes in over 40 colours. Its nose is usually short and snub. The large round eyes can be blue, copper, green, hazel or odd-eye.

Although the first documented evidence of Persian cats in Europe was in 1620 when Pietro della Valle imported them to Italy from Persia, now Iran, Persian cats from Turkey are known to have been in France in the 1500s. The cats from Persia were grey while those from Turkey were white and cross-breeding between the two was common. In the 19th century the Blue Persian was a must-have for the wealthy; and the blue is still popular in the British Isles. Queen Victoria was a proud owner of a blue. In 1871 a black smoke Persian – a type said to date back to the 1860s – was proudly exhibited at London's Crystal Palace cat show.

This is a cat for all the family – sweet, gentle and oh so laid back.

27

Pixie-Bob

Weight:
5.4 to 7.7 kg (12–17 lb)

Lifespan:
12 to 13 years

Description

The coat of the heavily built Pixie-Bob can be long or short. The colours include 'cool-toned' grey and black, patterned from spots to stripes, and 'warm-toned' brown, gold and russet with spots or stripes. The eyes are gold or gooseberry-green.

The Pixie-Bobs resemble the North American Bobcat. The story began in 1985 when the owner of a short-tailed polydactyl (see Cat Talk, at the end of this book) barn cat rescued the animal from a ferocious fight with a coastal red bobcat. Her reward was a litter of kittens which included a polydactyl male. This kitten so intrigued breeder Carol Ann Brewer from Washington that she bought it. After much research into polydactyl breeds and how they occurred, and with the help of two other cats with the same trait, a female bobtail, Pixie, was produced and gave her name to the breed. Is there any connection with other bob-tailed breeds such as the Manx? Definitely not?

Highly intelligent, very sociable and enjoy playing fetch.

28

RagaMuffin

Weight:
4.5 to 9 kg (10–20 lb)

Lifespan:
12 to 16 years

Description

RagaMuffin is a large, muscular, heavy breed with a dense, silky coat in every colour and pattern, with a ruff around the neck and face. The fur increases in length toward the tummy, finishing with large fluffy knickerbockers and a bottle-brush tail. The large, round, expressive eyes can be amber, blue, green, gold, hazel and odd-colour.

The RagaMuffin has the Ragdoll as an ancestor. In the 1990s a number of Ragdoll breeders, increasingly frustrated at a multitude of restrictions, used the Ragdoll as the basis for a new breed. The first RagaMuffins were out-crossed with other breeds including, so I understand, Persian and Himalayan, introducing a wider range of colours and patterns. The RagaMuffin takes up to five years to reach maturity.

The RagaMuffins are family cats, intelligent and playful companions, happy to sit on your lap and watch TV or chase a ball.

29

Ragdoll

Weight:
4 to 9 kg (8.8–20 lb)

Lifespan:
12 to 17 years

Description

One of the largest domestic cats, the Ragdoll has a silky plush coat that comes in six colours – seal, chocolate, flame, blue, lilac and cream. There are three patterns: colourpoint, like a Siamese, mitted (white gloves, boots and chin) and bi-colour. It has large, beautiful blue eyes.

Josephine, a pure white long-haired, is believed to be the mother of all Ragdoll cats. Josephine was hit by a car and taken to the vet. On return home, the cat was very docile and when picked up became limp in your arms, which was not the case before the accident. Ann Baker, a cat breeder, insisted the cat's genes had been altered at the hospital. Ann took the unusual step of patenting the Ragdoll name and took extremely strict control on anyone wishing to register the breed.

The breeding programme brought out the well-loved traits of the Ragdoll, those affectionate, intelligent and gentle creatures.

30

Russian Blue

Weight:
3.2 to 5.4 kg (7–12 lb)

Lifespan:
10 to 15 years

Description

The bluish-grey, thick, plush double coat consists of a short downy under coat, equal in length to the guard hairs, and a top coat. The blue hairs are tipped with silver and the nose is blue. The tail has almost invisible stripes. The almond-shaped, emerald-green eyes are slanted slightly upwards at the outer corners.

This naturally occurring, quiet, gentle and intelligent cat is believed to have originated in the port of Arkhangelsk (Archangel), Russia where their ancestors graced the palaces of Russian royalty. In the mid 19th century sailors brought them to Europe and they became favoured by Queen Victoria. The Second World War had a disastrous effect on breed numbers and to avoid extinction they were crossed with the Siamese. However, this introduced unwelcome traits, so this bloodline has now been removed from the Russian Blue make-up.

The child-friendly Russian Blue develops a deep personal bond with their family.

31

Savannah

Weight:
5.9 to 9 kg (13–20 lb)

Lifespan:
10 to 15 years

Description

The coat of the Savannah has dark brown/black spots on a background shade of brown, silver, black or black smoke. The over coat is slightly coarse to the touch and the under coat is soft. The Savannah's ears are large with rounded tops; the eyes are rich yellow, green, golden or caramel-brown. The legs are long.

The Savannah is a relatively newcomer to the cat scene, the first kitten having shown its spots and stripes in 1986. Judee Frank, the breeder, crossed a serval cat of the African plains with a domestic cat, and all who have seen them say they are 'breath-takingly gorgeous,' Patrick Kelley bought one of the kittens and with Joyce Stroufe took on the task of developing this new breed. It was accepted for registration in 2001.

They are tall, lean and graceful with the ability to jump on high cupboards and cabinets and even open cupboard doors. As a bonus they will hide your socks and pens. They love water and a cuddle.

32

Scottish Fold

Weight:
2.6 to 6 kg (5.7–13.2 lb)

Lifespan:
12 to 15 years

Description

The Scottish Fold comes in most cat colours including black and white, blue and white, black smoke and white and calico. It has a well-rounded body with a soft dense coat, a round head with chubby cheeks and large, round wide-open eyes whose colour depends on the coat colour. There are long- and short-haired varieties. The ears are pointed and fold forward and downward.

This breed was created in the 1960s after a Scottish shepherd William Ross, spotted Susie, a barn cat with folded ears, when he was visiting a neighbour's farm. Shortly afterwards William and his wife obtained Snooks, one of Susie's white female kittens and started a breeding programme. Susie is the mother of all true-bred Scottish Fold. In 1970 three of Snooks' kittens were sent to America and in 1978 the Cat Fanciers' Association granted the breed championship status. It became 8th in the top ten most popular breeds.

Not bad for a barn cat from Coupar Angus.

33

Selkirk Rex

Weight:
3 to 5 kg (6.6–11 lb)

Lifespan:
10 to 15 years

Description

Selkirk Rex comes in many colours. Its thick, dense coat is covered in loose ringlets that feel soft and plush to the touch. The head is round with chubby cheeks, the whiskers are curly or broken. The large round eyes can be any colour.

The Selkirk Rex has a permanent bad hair day. It originates from Montana in the United States where, in 1987, a curly haired kitten, later named Miss DePesto, was found in the litter of a rescued domestic cat. Miss DePesto is the mother of the breed. When she was bred with a black Persian male, half of her litter were curly. They were in turn crossed with the British and American Shorthair and the Exotic Shorthair. The Selkirk Rex can be long-haired with loose curls or short-haired with tighter curls. Selkirk was the family name of the breeder's step-father.

Good with children and the elderly, these perfect pets are, like me, patient, tolerant and loving.

34

Siamese

Weight:
3.2 to 6.4 kg (7–14 lb)

Lifespan:
11 to 15 years

Description

The main colours of the short glossy coat are seal, chocolate, blue and lilac, all with many variations. The Siamese has large pointed ears and deep blue almond-shaped eyes.

There are many myths and legends surrounding the Siamese cat from Siam, now Thailand. It is said they were born on the Ark. Records show the breed was in existence in the 14th century where they lived a pampered and privileged life in the palaces of royalty and noblemen. When their owners died the Siamese cat became the home and guardian of their souls, and was even more pampered. The first pair to arrive in the British Isles was in 1884, care of the British Consul-General in Bangkok, Edward Blencowe Gould, as a gift for his sister, Lilian Jane Veley. She became co-founder of the Siamese Cat Club.

This graceful, intelligent and affectionate cat has been 'improved' to create a sleeker, fine-boned breed. Is it an improvement? I will leave that for you to judge.

35

Siberian

Weight:
4.5 to 9 kg (9.9–20 lb)

Lifespan:
11 to 15 years

This breed comes in all colours including tabby and tortoiseshell with 124 variations in all. Hallmarks are a long, dense, water-resistant triple coat, a ruff, fluffy breeches and a bushy tail. The eyes are copper to green.

The Siberian originated in Russia over a thousand years ago and is believed to be the ancestor of all modern long-haired cats. The Siberians were bred as watch-cats in Russian monasteries. During the Communist regime the keeping of pets was forbidden and the Siberian became feral, living wild in the streets and countryside until the regime collapsed and they were taken in and domesticated. Breeding to create a pedigree began in 1987 and the first Siberian to put its paws on British soil was in 2002.

It will be no surprise that the Siberian is a hardy and healthy breed, but it is also gentle, affectionate and intelligent. It loves to play fetch, curl up on your lap and will join you in bed, given the chance.

36

Singapura

Weight:
1.8 to 3.5 kg (4–8 lb)

Lifespan:
11 to 15 years

The Singapura has a fine silky coat that is sepia brown or soft, golden ivory. It is ticked, each hair having bands of different colours. The ears are wide and deep. The large open eyes are hazel, green or yellow with a dark outline. It is one of the smallest breeds.

There has been considerable controversy about the beginning of the Singapura. The original claim made by Tommy and Hal Meadow is that while they were working in Singapore they found three distinctive 'drain cats' that they brought back to the United States. They started a breeding programme and were eventually joined by Catherine MacQuarrie and others. After years of hard work the breed was finally accepted for registration in 1981. However, the original Meadows account has been challenged.

So, is this a natural or a designer breed? Who cares. This intelligent, mischievous and loving cat is a joy to be around.

37

Snowshoe

Weight:
2.5 to 5.5 kg (5.4–12 lb)

Lifespan:
10 to 14 years

The short glossy coat is similar to that of the the Siamese as are the coat colours: seal, blue, chocolate, lilac, red and cream. Snowshoe has an inverted v-pattern on the lower part of its face, blue eyes and four white paws.

A rare breed, developed in the1960s by American breeder Dorothy Hinds-Daugherty. In a litter of Siamese kittens three had all-white paws so a breeding programme was started to reproduce this blip of nature. The first cross was with a bi-colour American Shorthair, and other crosses followed. Dorothy worked hard to promote the breed, now called the Snowshoe because of its white paws, with only partial success. She eventually abandoned the breeding programme and handed the reins to Vikki Olander who struggled to keep the breed going and in the public eye. Vikki was eventually joined by George Kuhnell and Jim Hoffman, and the Snowshoe was finally recognised by the International Cat Association in 1993.

The calm and gentle Snowshoe is definitely a lap cat.

38

Somali

Weight:

3.6 to 5.4 kg (8–12 lb)

Lifespan:

11 to 16 years

Description

The Somali usually has a golden-brown coat ticked with black and exuberant tufts and a superb bushy tail. The ears are large with a broad base; the eyes are green or gold with a dark surrounding ring.

As with so many breeds, the question where and when they appeared cannot be easily answered. In the early to mid 20th century many breeds were on the point of extinction, the casualties of two world wars. The breeders of the Abyssinian were forced to cross-breed to keep the breed alive. A number of the resultant offspring were long-haired and unwanted. In 1963 Mary Mailing, a Canadian Aby breeder, put a long-haired offspring in a show as a practical joke. The judge, Ken McGill, did not see the joke, only a beautiful cat. Starting with a cat from Mary he started to breed the gorgeous long-haired Somali. It is the oldest Somali line in Canada.

The 'fox cat' loves being around people.

39

Sphynx

Weight:
3.5 to 7 kg (7.7–15.4 lb)

Lifespan:
8 to 15 years

Description

The Sphynx has a skin that feels like warm chamois. It can be in all the usual colours including chocolate, black, blue tortoiseshell and lilac. It has a 'rat like' tail. The almond-shaped eyes are mainly green, blue and hazel.

In past years hairless cats have appeared in many countries; the Aztecs are reputed to have bred them. Despite their appearance, they are covered with a fine peach-like fuzz. The modern Sphynx began its life in Toronto, Canada in 1966 with a black-and-white domestic short-haired cat giving birth to a litter which included one hairless male. It was given the name of Prune, and subsequent breeding using Prune created more hairless kittens. The European Sphynx was created from two kittens exported to Holland from Canada. Known originally as Moonstones or Canadian Hairless, they were re-named the Sphynx because of their similarity to an Egyptian cat statue in the Louvre.

They love to be a part of the everyday household life, and are very affectionate and intelligent.

40

Tonkinese

Weight:
2.5 to 5.5 kg (5.5–12 lb)

Lifespan:
15 to 18 years

Description

The coat comes in four basic colours – brown, blue, chocolate and lilac – with three to four patterns to each colour. The eyes are blue, aquamarine and yellow-green.

There is a belief amongst some breeders that the Tonkinese was around in the 1800s. However, most breeders accept that the modern Tonk was created in 1930, a cross of the Siamese and Burmese, retaining the beautiful dark coat of the Burmese but with the point pattern – although darker – of the Siamese. The matriarch of the breed is Wong Mau, a legend in the Tonkinese breeder's world, owned by Joseph Cheesman Thompson, a breeder of Burmese cats. The tireless work of a Canadian breeder, Margaret Conroy, in conjunction with two American breeders, was the driving force in developing the breed as known today, and having it recognised by the Canadian Cat Association in 1974. The breed was recognised by the British and Australian cat registries in the 1980s.

This playful animal loves company.

41

Turkish Angora

Weight:
3 to 8.5 kg (6.6–19 lb)

Lifespan:
9 to 15 years

Description

This slender, elegant breed has a long-haired silky coat that is mainly white but also black, blue, red, cream and bi-colour. Its ears are large and close-set. The eyes are blue, green, gold, copper or odd-eyed.

The Turkish Angora is one of the oldest natural breeds of long-haired cats in the world. They arrived in Britain and France via Russia, Asia Minor and Persia, now Iran, in the 1500s but are believed to have been in Europe, courtesy of the Crusaders, at least a hundred years before that. The Victorians used the Turkish Angora to improve the coat of the Persian cat and this thoughtless breeding pushed the Angora to the point of extinction. In the early 20th century the Ankara zoo, in collaboration with the Turkish government, set up a breeding programme to preserve the odd-eyed pure white Angora which had by now been recognised as a national treasure.

They are intelligent, loving and playful, an ideal family pet.

Cat Talk

When you become involved with the world of cats you realise how varied and interesting they are. Here are explanations of some of the terms used in this book as well as just one or two of the many fascinating details about them.

Points The coats of some cats, for example the Siamese, have extremities that are darker than the main coat colour. The main point areas are face, ears, feet and tail.

Coats Most breeds of cats have three layers of coats. The under coat is very fine and perhaps 1 cm long. There is a middle layer of coarser hair and then the top coat or 'guard hairs'. In a short-haired cat the outer coat is typically 5 cm long; in a longhair it is twice that or more.

Some cats appear to have no coat, or just a downy undercoat.

Ticking As in the Abyssinian, the hairs of the coat are lighter at the base, becoming darker in bands towards the top.

Rex This refers to curly or otherwise unusual fur in, for instance, the Cornish Rex. The story goes that the name was coined when King Albert 1st of Belgium entered some curly haired rabbits in a show. The organisers should have rejected the animals but, to avoid offending the king, wrote 'Rex' (Latin for 'king') beside them.

Whiskers A cat has about 24 whiskers, four rows each side. The upper two rows can move independently of the bottom two. The whiskers are used for measuring distances. Watch your own cat. Do its whiskers lie flat when it is defensive but come forward when it is feeling friendly?

Eyes Yes, cats see better than us in the dark. They have a *tapetum lucidum*, a reflective layer behind the retina that sends light that passes through the retina back into the eye.

Odd-eye The odd-eye cat has eyes of different colours: one blue, the other yellow, brown or green.

Polydactyl claws Most cats have five claws on each front paw and four or five on each rear paw. However, some breeds, such as Maine Coon and Pixie-Bob, have inherited a mutation because of which they may have extra toes.

Litters These are kittens born at the same time to the same mother. Although the average number is about 4–6 per litter, this can vary widely, from one to ten or more.

Breed standards Cat breed associations set up lists of the ideal characteristics for the breed in an attempt to ensure that they remain distinctive and continue to show traits that the breeders approve.

How fast can a cat run? They can usually manage up to about 48 kilometres per hour (30 mph), though the Egyptian Mau can exceed that.

Talk Besides the well-known meow and purr, cats make chirrups, growls and hisses. Some breeds, such as the Burmese, are said to be more talkative than others.